A N.
DAWNING

A COMPILATION OF PRAISE, PRAYER, AND PSALMS OF THANKSGIVING

By Bobbie Hansen-Stewart

Independently Published

Kindle/Amazon

ISBN: 9798567301593

Bobbie Hansen-Stewart, Compiling

BJStewart51@Gmail.com

HoltPublishing4U@gmail.com

Unless otherwise noted, Scripture quotations are from The Holy Bible, King James Version, (KJV) or New King James Version (NKJV).

TO THE READER

A NEW DAY DAWNING is a book of life changing Bible scripture which shares the good news of Jesus Christ with our world today. Jesus offers a new beginning; a fresh start and promises a **life change** for those who feel broken and alone both spiritually and physically.

Hopefully, the compilation of *Praise, Prayer, and Psalms of Thanksgiving* scripture quotations will help readers comprehend the Bible and apply it to their lives; leading them to a better understanding of God and His Word, while finding peace in His presence.

THE EIGHT BEATITUDES OF JESUS

"Blessed are the poor in spirit,
for theirs is the kingdom of heaven.

Blessed are they who mourn,
for they shall be comforted.

Blessed are the meek,
for they shall inherit the earth.

Blessed are they who hunger and thirst for
righteousness,
for they shall be satisfied.

Blessed are the merciful,
for they shall obtain mercy.

Blessed are the pure of heart,
for they shall see God.

Blessed are the peacemakers,
for they shall be called children of God.

Blessed are they who are persecuted for the sake of
righteousness, for theirs is the kingdom of heaven."

Matthew 5:3-10

Lord Jesus Saves

INTRODUCTION

During my wilderness walk, the Holy Spirit would awaken my soul for prayer and meditation each day on the wings of the dawn. It seemed I was praying day and night, and finding peace in His presence. The more I prayed, meditated and studied God's word His Presence became more real in my life. As I began to grow spiritually a realization was also growing that God is always present and aware of our needs. God is our Security. He surrounds us with His presence and fills us with His Spirit. God is our praise, prayer, and psalms of thanksgiving.

The other night I dreamed of lying on the seashore, with the waves splashing over me, washing me out to sea. I felt as if there was no strength left within me. I could feel the wet sand beneath me slowly-slowly carrying me away. *As a New Day* was *Dawning,* and the sun was breaking through the thick, dark, tempestuous clouds, an "Angel" came walking along the sea shore lifting me from the splashing, rough waves and the raging, stormy sea.

The "Angel" lovingly carried me, placing me on dry ground behind a large boulder. I could feel the wind blowing ever so gently across my face, moving the clouds of doom and filling my lungs with *Praise, Prayer, and Psalms of Thanksgiving.*

TABLE OF CONTENTS

PRAISE, PRAYER, AND PSALMS OF THANKSGIVING

In the beginning '*GOD*' created the heaven and the earth.   Genesis 1:1

The rainbow shall be in the cloud, and I will look on it to remember the everlasting covenant between God and every living creature of all flesh that is upon the earth.   Genesis 9:16

Shortly before dawn Jesus went out to them, walking on the water. When the disciples saw him walking on the water, they were terrified. "It's a ghost," they said, and cried out in fear. But Jesus immediately said to them: "Take courage! It is I. Do not be afraid." "Lord, if it's you," Peter replied, "tell me to come to you on the water." "Come," he said. Then Peter got down out of the boat, walked on the water and came toward Jesus. When Peter saw the wind and waves, he was afraid and beginning to sink, cried out, "Lord, save me.!" Immediately Jesus reached out his hand and caught him. "You of little faith, he said, "Why did you doubt?"   Matthew 14: 25-31

When you feel like you're overwhelmed and drowning in everyday circumstances, just like Peter, cry out to Jesus, Remember, Our God Walks On Water.

"If you abide in me, and my words abide in you, ask whatever you wish, and it will be done for you. My Father is glorified by this, that you bear much fruit, and so prove to be my disciples."   John 15:7-8

Therefore, my dear brothers and sisters, be steadfast, immovable, always abounding in the work of the Lord, knowing that your labor in the Lord, is not in vain.   1 Corinthians 15:58

And Moses said to the people, "Do not be afraid, stand still and see the salvation of the Lord, which He will accomplish for you today. For the Egyptians whom you see today, you shall see again no more forever. The Lord will fight for you, and you shall hold your peace."   Exodus 14:13-14

You have seen what I did to the Egyptians, and how I bore you on eagles' wings and brought you to myself. Now therefore, if you will indeed obey my voice and keep my covenant, then you shall be a special treasure to me above all people; for all the earth is mine.   Exodus 19: 4-5

Fear not, I am thy shield, and thy exceeding great reward   Genesis 15:1

 Behold, I send an Angel before you to keep you in the way and to bring you into the place which I have prepared. Beware of him and obey his voice; do not provoke him, for he will not pardon your transgressions; for my name is in him. But if you indeed obey his voice and do all that I speak, then I will be an enemy to your enemies and an adversary to your adversaries.   Exodus 23:20-22

So, the Lord said to Moses, "I will also do this thing that you have spoken; for you have found grace in my   sight,   and   I   know   you   by   name."
                              Exodus 33:17

And he has filled him with the Spirit of God, in wisdom and understanding, in knowledge and all manner of workmanship.   Exodus 35:31

Speak to all the congregation of the children of Israel, and say to them: You shall be holy; for I the Lord your God am holy.   Leviticus 19:2

The Lord bless you, and keep you; The Lord make his face shine upon you, and be gracious unto you; The Lord lift up his countenance upon you, and give you peace; they shall put my name upon you; and I will bless you.   Numbers 6:22-27

May the Lord, the God of the spirits of all flesh, appoint a man over the congregation, who will go out and come in before them, and who will lead them out and bring them in, so that the congregation of the Lord will not be like sheep which have no shepherd.   Numbers 27:16-17

This book of the law shall not depart from your mouth, but you shall meditate in it day and night, that you may observe to do according to all that is written in it. For then you will make your way prosperous, and then you will have good success. Have I not commanded you? Be strong and of a good courage; do not be afraid, nor be dismayed, for the Lord your God is with you wherever you go.

Joshua 1:8-10

Then Joshua spoke to the Lord in the day when the Lord delivered up the Amorites before the sons of Israel, and he said in the sight of Israel, "Sun, stand still at Gibeon, and you, moon, in the valley of Aijalon." So, the sun stood still, and the moon stopped, until the nation avenged themselves of their enemies, as it is written in the book of Jashar. The sun stopped in the middle of the sky and did not hasten to go down for about a whole day.

Joshua 10:12-13

But from there you will seek the Lord your God, and you will find Him if you seek Him with all your heart and with all your soul. When you are in distress, and all these things come upon you in the latter days, when you turn to the Lord your God and obey His voice (for the Lord your God is a merciful God), He will not forsake you nor destroy you, nor forget the covenant of your fathers which He swore to them. Deuteronomy 4:29-31

We have this hope as an anchor for the soul, firm and secure. It enters the inner sanctuary behind the curtain, where our forerunner, Jesus, has entered on our behalf. He has become a high priest forever, in the order of Melchizedek.   Hebrews 6:19-20

Therefore know that the Lord your God, He is God, the faithful God who keeps covenant and mercy for a thousand generations with those who love him and keep his commandments; and he repays those who hate him to their face, to destroy them. He will not be slack with him who hates him; He will repay him to his face.   Therefore, you shall keep the commandment, the statutes, and the judgments which I command you today, to observe them.

Deuteronomy 7:9-11

HANNAH'S PRAYERS

She made a vow and said, "O Lord of hosts, if you will indeed look on the affliction of your maidservant and remember me, and not forget your maidservant, but will give your maidservant a son, then I will give him to the Lord all the days of his life, and a razor shall never come on his head."

1 Samuel 1:11

Now Hannah spoke in her heart; only her lips moved, but her voice was not heard. Therefore, Eli thought she was drunk. 1 Samuel 1:13

So, in the course of time Hannah became pregnant and gave birth to a son. She named him Samuel, saying, "Because I asked the Lord for him."

1 Samuel 1:20

Hannah's Song of Thanksgiving

Then Hannah prayed and said, "My heart exalts in the Lord; my horn is exalted in the Lord, my mouth speaks boldly against my enemies, because I rejoice in your salvation. There is no one holy like the Lord, indeed, there is no one besides you; there is no Rock like our God. 1 Samuel 2: 1-2

Then Samson called to the Lord and said, "O Lord God, please remember me and please strengthen me just this time, O God, that I may at once be avenged of the Philistines for my two eyes." Then Samson reached toward the two central pillars on which the temple stood, bracing himself against them, his right hand on the one and his left hand on the other, Samson said, "Let me die with the Philistines!" then he pushed with all his might, and down came the temple on the rulers and all the people in it. Thus he killed many more when he died than while he lived.

Judges 16:28-30

I go the way of all the earth; be strong, therefore, and prove yourself a man, and keep the charge of the Lord your God: to walk in His ways, to keep His statutes, His commandments, and His judgments, and His testimonies, as it is written in the Law of Moses, that you may prosper in all that you do and wherever you turn;   1 Kings 2:2-3

At the time of the offering of the evening sacrifice, Elijah the prophet came near and said, "O Lord, the God of Abraham, Isaac and Israel, today let it be known that you are God in Israel and that I am your servant and I have done all these things at your word.   1Kings 18:36

Then the fire of the Lord fell and consumed the burnt offering and the wood and the stones and the dust, and licked up the water that was in the trench.   1 Kings 18:38

When they had crossed over, Elijah said to Elisha, "Ask what I shall do for you before I am taken from you," and Elisha said, "Please, let a double portion of your spirit be upon me."   2 Kings 2:9

He also took up the mantel of Elijah that had fallen from him, and went back and stood by the bank of the Jordan.   Then he took the mantel of Elijah that had fallen from him, and struck the water, and said, "Where is the Lord God of Elijah?" And when he had struck the water, it was divided this way and that; and Elisha crossed over.   2 Kings 2: 13-14

Blessed be the Lord, who has given rest to His people Israel, according to all that He promised. There has not failed one word of all His good promise, which He promised through His servant Moses.   1Kings 8:56

Our faith is not in the wisdom of men, but in the power of God.

Behold, this day I am going the way of all the earth, and you know in all your hearts and in all your souls that not one thing has failed of all the good things which the Lord your God spoke concerning you. All have come to pass for you; not one word of them has failed.   Joshua 23:14

And if it seems evil to you to serve the Lord, choose for yourselves this day whom you will serve, whether the gods which your fathers served that were on the other side of the river, or the gods of the Amorites, in whose land you dwell. But as for me and my house, we will serve the Lord.

Joshua 24:15

May the Lord our God be with us as he was with our fathers; may he not leave us nor forsake us, that he may incline our hearts to himself, to walk in all his ways, and to keep his commandments and his statutes and his judgments, which he commanded our fathers.   1 Kings 8: 57-58

And he stretched himself upon the child three times, and cried unto the Lord, and said, O Lord my God, I pray, let this child's soul come into him again. And the Lord heard the voice of Elijah; and the soul of the child came into him again, and he revived.

1 Kings 17:21-22

Now you have been pleased to bless the house of your servant, that it may continue before you forever; for you have blessed it, O Lord, and it shall be blessed forever.   1 Chronicles 17:27

As for you, my son *Solomon,* know the God of your father, and serve Him with a loyal heart and with a willing mind; for the Lord searches all hearts and understands all the intent of the thoughts. If you seek Him, He will be found by you; but if you forsake Him, He will cast you off forever.

1 Chronicles 28:9

For the eyes of the Lord run to and fro throughout the whole earth, to show Himself strong on behalf of those whose heart is loyal to Him. In this you have done foolishly; therefore from now on you shall have wars.   2 Chronicles 16:9

For Ezra had prepared his heart to seek the law of the Lord, and to do it, and to teach in Israel statues and judgments.   Ezra 7:10

And to man He said, Behold, the fear of the Lord, that is wisdom, and to depart from evil is understanding.   Job 28:28

Great men are not always wise, nor do the aged always understand justice.   Job 32:9

For the ear tests words as the mouth tastes food.
                                                              Job 34:3

All the while my breath is in me, and the spirit of God is in my nostrils; my lips shall not speak wickedness, nor my tongue utter deceit. God forbid that I should justify you: till I die I will not remove mine integrity from me.   Job 27:3-6

Who so ever drinks of the water that I shall give him will never thirst. But the water that I shall give him will become in him a fountain of water springing up into everlasting life.   John 4:14

The hour is coming, and now is, when the true worshipers will worship the Father in spirit and truth; for the Father is seeking such to worship him. God is Spirit, and those who worship him must worship in spirit and truth.   John 4:23-24

Do not labor for the food which perishes, but for the food which endures to everlasting life, which the Son of Man will give you, because God the Father has set his seal on Him.   John 6:27

WE PRAISE HIM IN THE SANCTUARY

THE GLORY OF THE LORD FILLED THE HOUSE OF GOD

PRAISE

It came to pass, when the trumpeters and singers were as one, to make one sound to be heard in praising and thanking the Lord, and when they lifted up their voice with the trumpets and cymbals and instruments of music, and praised the Lord, saying; "For He is good, for His mercy endures forever," that the house, the house of the Lord, was filled with a cloud, so that the priests could not continue ministering because of the cloud; for the glory of the Lord filled the house of God.

2 Chronicles 5: 13-14

And when they began to sing and to praise, the Lord set an ambush against the children of Ammon, Moab, and Mount Seir, which were come against Judah; and they were defeated.   2 Chronicles 20:22

I urge, then first of all, that petitions, prayers, intercession and thanksgiving be made for all people-for kings and all those in authority, that we may live peaceful and quite lives in all godliness and holiness. This is good, and pleases God our

Savior, who wants all people to be saved and to come to a knowledge of the truth. For there is one God and one mediator between God and mankind, the man Christ Jesus, who gave himself as a ransom for all people.   1 Timothy 2: 1-6

"Therefore, having been justified by faith, we have peace with God through our Lord Jesus Christ, through whom also we have access by faith into this grace in which we stand, and rejoice in hope of the glory of God. And not only that, but we also glory in tribulations, knowing that tribulation produces perseverance; and perseverance, character; and character, hope. Now hope does not disappoint, because the love of God has been poured out in our hearts by the Holy Spirit who was given to us. For when we were still without strength, in due time Christ died for the ungodly."   Romans 5:1-6

If the Lord delights in us, then He will bring us into this land and give it to us, a land which flows with milk and honey.   Numbers 14:8

Now may the God of patience and comfort grant you to be like-minded toward one another, according to Christ Jesus, that you may with one mind and one mouth glorify the God and Father of our Lord Jesus Christ. Therefore receive one another, just as Christ also received us, to the glory of God. Romans 15:5-7

To appoint unto them that mourn in Zion, to give unto them beauty for ashes, the oil of joy for mourning, the garment of praise for the spirit of heaviness; that they might be called trees of righteousness, the planting of the Lord, that he might be glorified. Isaiah 61:3

JESUS' PRAYERS

Jesus Prays for Himself

Jesus spoke these words, lifted up His eyes to heaven, and said: "Father, the hour has come. Glorify Your Son, that Your Son also may glorify you, as you have given him authority over all flesh, that he should give eternal life to as many as you have given him. And this is eternal life, that they may know you, the only true God, and Jesus Christ whom you have sent. I have glorified you on the earth. I have finished the work which you have given me to do. And now, O Father, glorify me together with yourself, with the glory which I had with you before the world was.   John 17: 1-5

Jesus Prays for His Followers

I have manifested your name to the ones whom you have given me out of the world. They were yours, you gave them to me, and they have kept your word. Now they have known that all things which you have given me are from you. For I have given to them the words which you have given me; and they have received them, and know surely that I came forth from you; and they have believed that you sent me.   John 17: 6-8

Jesus Prays for His Disciples

I pray for them. I do not pray for the world but for those whom you have given me, for they are yours. And all mine are yours, and yours are mine, and I am glorified in them. Now I am no longer in the world, but these are in the world, and I come to you. Holy Father, keep through your name those whom you have given me that they may be one as we are. While I was with them in the world, I kept them in your name. Those whom you gave me I have kept; and none of them is lost except the son of perdition, that the Scripture might be fulfilled. But now I come to you, and these things I speak in the world, that they may have my joy fulfilled in themselves. I have given them your word; and the world has hated them because they are not of the world, just as I am not of the world. Sanctify them by your truth. Your word is truth. As you sent me into the world, I also have sent them into the world. And for their sakes I sanctify myself, that they also may be sanctified by the truth.   John 17:6-19

Jesus Prays for all Believers

I do not pray for these alone, but also for those who will believe in me through their word; that they all may be one, as you, Father, are in me, and I in you; that they also may be one in us, that the world may believe that you sent me. And the glory which you gave me I have given them, that they may be one just as we are one: I in them, and you in me; that they may be made perfect in one, and that the world may know that you have sent me, and have loved them as you have loved me.

Father, I desire that they also whom you gave me may be with me where I am, that they may behold my glory which you have given me; for you loved me before the foundation of the world. O righteous Father! The world has not known you, but I have known you; and these have known that you sent me. And I have declared to them your name, and will declare it, that the love with which you loved me may be in them, and I in them." John 17: 20-26

Let the word of Christ dwell in you richly in all wisdom, teaching and admonishing one another in psalms and hymns and spiritual songs, singing with grace in your hearts to the Lord. And whatever you do in word or deed, do all in the name of the Lord Jesus, giving thanks to God the Father through Him. Colossians 3:16-17

And you shall remember the Lord your God, for it is he who gives you power to get wealth, that he may establish his covenant which he swore to your fathers, as it is this day. Deuteronomy 8:18

And now, (Israel), what does the Lord your God require of you, but to fear the Lord your God, to walk in all his ways and to love him, to serve the Lord your God with all your heart and with all your soul. Deuteronomy 10:12

You shall not pervert justice; you shall not show partiality, nor take a bribe, for a bribe blinds the eyes of the wise and twists the words of the righteous. Deuteronomy 16:19

He is your praise, and he is your God, who has done for you these great and awesome things which your eyes have seen. Deuteronomy 10:21

We know prayer makes a difference; our prayers and our tears touch the heart of God. Jesus still weeps with us today, as He wept with Mary and Martha at the tomb of Lazarus. John 11:35

SPIRITUAL FREEDOM IS A BLESSING

BLESSINGS

1-Now it shall come to pass, if you diligently obey the voice of the Lord your God, to observe carefully all his commandments which I command you today, that the Lord your God will set you high above all nations of the earth.   Deuteronomy 28:1

2-And all these blessings shall come upon you and overtake you, because you obey the voice of the Lord your God.

3-Blessed shall you be in the city, and blessed shall you be in the field.

4-Blessed shall be the fruit of your body, and the fruit of your ground and the fruit of your cattle, the increase of the flocks of your sheep.

5-Blessed shall be your basket and your store.

6-Blessed shall you be when you come in, and blessed shall you be when you go out.

7-The Lord shall cause your enemies that rise up against you to be smitten before your face: they shall come out against you one way, and flee before you seven ways.

8-The Lord shall command the blessing upon you in your storehouses, and in all that you set your hand unto; and he shall bless you in the land which the Lord your God gives you.

9-The Lord shall establish you a holy people unto Himself, as he hath sworn unto you, if you shall keep the commandments of the Lord your God, and walk in his ways.

10-All people of the earth shall see that you are called by the name of the Lord; and they shall be afraid of you.

11-The Lord shall make you plenteous in goods, in the fruit of your body, and in the fruit of your cattle, and in the fruit of your ground, in the land which the Lord sware unto your fathers to give you.

12-The Lord shall open unto you his good treasure, the heaven to give the rain unto your land in his season, and to bless all the work of your hand: and you shall lend to many nations, and you shall not borrow.   Deuteronomy 28:12

13-The Lord shall make you the head, and not the tail; you shall be above only, and you shall not be beneath; if you hearken unto the commandments of the Lord your God, which I command you this day, to observe and to do them.

14-You shall not go aside from any of the words which I command you this day, to the right hand, or to the left, to go after other gods to serve them.

Deuteronomy 28:14

And the Lord your God will circumcise your heart and the heart of your descendants, to love the Lord your God with all your heart and with all your soul that you may live.

Deuteronomy 30:6

But the word is very near you, in your mouth and in your heart, that you may do it.   Deuteronomy 30:14

Be strong and of good courage, do not fear nor be afraid of them; for the Lord your God, he is the One who goes with you.   He will not leave you nor forsake you.   Deuteronomy 31:6

For I proclaim the name of the Lord: Ascribe greatness to our God.   He is the Rock, his work is perfect; for all his ways are justice, A God of truth and without injustice; righteous and upright is he.
Deuteronomy 32:3-4

Now therefore, let it please you to bless the house of your servant, that it may continue before you forever; for you, O Lord God, have spoken it, and with your blessing let the house of your servant be blessed forever."   2 Samuel 7:29

He sent from above, he took me; he drew me out of many waters; He delivered me from my strong enemy, and from them that hated me; for they were too strong for me.   2 Samuel 22:17-18

Blessed is the man that walks not in the counsel of the ungodly, nor stands in the way of sinners, nor sits in the seat of the scornful. But his delight is in the law of the Lord; and in his law he meditates day and night. And he shall be like a tree planted by the rivers of water, that brings forth his fruit in his season; his leaf also shall not wither, and whatsoever he does shall prosper.   Psalm 1:1-3

The ungodly are not so; but are like the chaff which the wind drives away. Therefore the ungodly shall not stand in the judgment, nor sinners in the congregation of the righteous. For the Lord knows the way of the righteous, but the way of the ungodly shall perish.   Psalm 1: 4-6

Give ear to my words, O Lord, consider my meditation. Give heed to the voice of my cry, my King and my God, for unto you will I pray. My voice you shall hear in the morning, O Lord; in the morning will I direct my prayer unto you, and will look up.   Psalm 5:1-3

O Lord, do not rebuke me in your anger, nor chasten me in your hot displeasure. Have mercy on me, O Lord, for I am weak; O Lord, heal me, for my bones are troubled.   My soul also is greatly troubled; But you, O Lord-how long?   Psalm 6:1-3

I will praise you, O Lord, with my whole heart; I will tell of all your marvelous works. I will be glad and rejoice in you; I will sing praise to your name, O Most High.   Psalm 9: 1-2

Bless the Lord, O my soul: and all that is within me, Bless his holy name. Bless the Lord, O my soul, and forget not all his benefits; who forgives all your iniquities; who heals all your diseases; who redeems your life from destruction; who crowns you with loving kindness and tender mercies; who satisfies your mouth with good things; so that your youth is renewed like the eagle's.   Psalm 103:1-5

Hold up my goings in your paths, that my footsteps may not slip.   Psalm 17:5

I will love you, O Lord, my strength. The Lord is my rock, and my fortress, and my deliverer; my God, my strength, in whom I will trust; my shield, and the horn of my salvation, my stronghold. I will call upon the Lord, who is worthy to be praised; so shall I be saved from my enemies.   Psalm 18: 1-3

He sent from above, He took me; He drew me out of many waters. He delivered me from my strong enemy, from those who hated me, for they were too strong for me.   Psalm 18:16-17

O Lord my God, in you I put my trust; save me from all those who persecute me; and deliver me.
                                                            Psalm 7:1

Thy testimonies have I taken as an heritage for ever: for they are the rejoicing of my heart.   I have inclined my heart to perform your statutes always, even unto the end.   Psalm 119: 111-112

You enlarged my path under me, so my feet did not slip.   Psalm 18:36

Let the words of my mouth, and the meditation of my heart, be acceptable in your sight, O Lord, my strength, and my redeemer.   Psalm 19:14

O Lord my God, in you I put my trust; save me from all those who persecute me; and deliver me.
                                                            Psalm 7:1

The Lord is my strength and my shield; my heart trusted in him, and I am helped; therefore my heart greatly rejoices; and with my song I will praise him.

The Lord is their strength, and he is the saving strength of his anointed. Psalm 28: 7-8

Lord God, you are my rock and my fortress, therefore, for thy name's sake lead me and guide me. Psalm 31:3

Love the Lord all you people for the Lord preserves the faithful and plentifully rewards the proud doer. Be of good courage and he shall strengthen your heart, all you that hope in the Lord. Psalm 31:23

Therefore let all the faithful pray to you while you may be found; surely the rising of the mighty waters will not reach them. Psalm 32:6

I will instruct you and teach you in the way you should go; I will guide you with my eye.

Psalms 32:8

I will bless the Lord at all times; his praise shall continually be in my mouth. My soul shall make its boast in the Lord: The humble shall hear of it and be glad. Oh, magnify the Lord with me, and let us exalt his name together. Psalm 34: 1-3

The eyes of the Lord are on the righteous, and his ears are attentive to their cry; but the face of the Lord is against those who do evil, to blot out their name from the earth. The righteous cry out, and the Lord hears them; he delivers them from all their troubles.   Psalm 34:15-17

Delight thyself also in the Lord and He shall give you the desires of your heart.   Psalm 37:4

The steps of a good man are ordered by the Lord:

 and he delights in his way. Though he fall, he shall not be utterly cast down: for the Lord upholds him with his hand. I have been young, and now am old; yet have I not seen the righteous forsaken, nor his seed begging bread.
Psalm 37: 23-25

Rest in the Lord, and wait patiently for him; fret not yourself because of him who prospers in his way, because of the man who brings wicked devises to pass. A little that a righteous man has is better than the riches of many wicked.   Psalm 37:7:16

Why are you cast down, O my soul? And why are you disquieted within me? Hope in God; for I shall yet praise him, The health of my countenance, and my God.   Psalm 42:11

Send out your light and your truth; Let them lead me; Let them bring me unto your holy hill, and to your tabernacles.   Psalm 43:3

Whoso offers praise glorifies me: and to him that orders his conversation aright will I show the salvation of God.   Psalm 50:23

Offer to God thanksgiving, and pay your vows to the Most High. Call upon me in the day of trouble; I will deliver you, and you shall glorify me.
                    Psalm 50:14-15

Evening, morning, and at noon I will pray, and cry aloud, and God shall hear my voice. He has redeemed my soul in peace from the battle that was against me, for there were many with me.
                    Psalm 55:17-18

In God I will praise his word, in God I have put my trust; I will not fear what flesh can do unto me.

Psalm 56:4

Hear my cry, O God, attend unto my prayer. From the end of the earth will I cry unto you, when my heart is overwhelmed; Lead me to the rock that is higher than I for you have been a shelter for me, A strong tower from the enemy.   Psalm 61:1-3

God, You are my God; Early will I seek you; my soul thirsts for you, my flesh longs for you in a dry and thirsty land where no water is; To see your power and your glory, so as I have seen you in the sanctuary. Because your loving kindness is better than life, my lips shall praise you; I will bless you while I live: I will lift up my hands in your name.

Psalm 63:1-4

Let my mouth be filled with your praise and with your honor all the day. Cast me not off in the time of old age; forsake me not when my strength fails.

Psalm 71:8-9

Better is one day in your courts than a thousand elsewhere; I would rather be a doorkeeper in the house of my God than dwell in the tents of the wicked. Psalm 84:10

For the Lord God is a sun and shield: The Lord will give grace and glory; No good thing will he withhold from them that walk uprightly.

Psalm 84:11

I will praise You, O Lord my God, with my whole heart; and I will glorify your name for evermore.

Psalm 86:12

But I am poor and sorrowful; let your salvation, O God, set me up on high. I will praise the name of God with a song, and will magnify him with thanksgiving. Psalm 69:29-30

Shout for joy to God, all the earth; Sing the glory of his name; Make his praise glorious. Say unto God, how awesome are you in your works: Through the greatness of your power shall your enemies submit themselves unto you. All the earth shall worship you, and shall sing unto you; they shall sing unto your name. Amen Psalm 66:1-4

Oh come, let us sing to the Lord! Let us shout joyfully to the Rock of our salvation. Let us come before his presence with thanksgiving; Let us shout joyfully to him with psalms. For the Lord is the great God, and the great King above all gods.

Psalm 95:1-3

MY MOUTH SHALL SPEAK THE PRAISE
OF THE LORD

BLESSING THE LORD IS WORSHIP

Bless the Lord, O my soul and all that is within me, bless his holy name. Bless the Lord, O my soul, and forget not all his benefits.   Psalm 103:1-2

Praise the Lord, all you nations; praise him, all you people, for his merciful kindness is great toward us; and the truth of the Lord endures forever.   Praise you the Lord.   Psalm 117:1-2

Sing unto the Lord a new song; sing unto the Lord, all the earth. Sing unto the Lord, bless His name; show forth his salvation from day to day.

Psalm 96:1-2

Give thanks unto the Lord; call upon his name; make known his deeds among the people.   Sing unto him, sing psalms unto him: talk you of all his wondrous works.   Glory you in his holy name; let the heart of them rejoice that seek the Lord.   Seek the Lord, and his strength; seek his face evermore.

Psalm: 105:1

I will greatly praise the Lord with my mouth; yes I will praise him among the multitude. Psalm 109:30

My soul melts for heaviness: strengthen thou me according unto your word.   Psalm 119:28

Sing unto the Lord a new song; sing unto the Lord, all the earth. Sing unto the Lord, bless his name; show forth his salvation from day to day.

Psalm 96:1-2

Praise the Lord, Praise, O you servants of the Lord, praise the name of the Lord. Blessed be the name of the Lord from this time forth and for evermore. From the rising of the sun unto the going down of the same the Lord's name is to be praised.

Psalm 113:1-3

The Lord is my strength and song, and he is become my salvation; he is my God, and I will prepare him an habitation; my father's God, and I will exalt him.

Exodus 15:2

Cause me to hear your loving kindness in the morning, for in thee do I trust: Cause me to know the way wherein I should walk; for I lift up my soul to you. Deliver me, O Lord, from my enemies; I flee unto you to hide me.   Psalm 143:8-9

Teach me to do your will; for you are my God; your spirit is good; lead me in the land of uprightness.
Psalm 143:10

I will exalt you, my God, O king; and I will bless your name forever and ever. Every day will I bless you; and I will praise your name forever and ever. Great is the Lord, and greatly to be praised; and His greatness is unsearchable.   Psalm145:1-3

My mouth shall speak the praise of the Lord: and let all flesh bless his holy name forever and ever.
Psalm 145:21

For you shall go out with joy, and be led forth with peace: the mountains and the hills shall break forth before you into singing, and all the trees of the field shall clap their hands.   Isaiah 55:12

Praise the Lord. Praise God in His sanctuary: Praise Him in the firmament of His power. Praise Him for his mighty acts: Praise Him according to His excellent greatness. Praise Him with the sound of the trumpet: Praise Him with the psaltery and harp.

Praise Him with the timbrel and dance, Praise Him with stringed instruments and organs. Praise Him upon the loud cymbals; Praise Him upon the high sounding cymbals. Let everything that has breath praise the Lord. Praise you the Lord.

Psalms 150:1-6

And in that day you will say, O Lord, I will praise you, though you were angry with me, your anger is turned away, and you comforted me. Behold, God is my salvation; I will trust, and not be afraid: for the Lord, JEHOVAH, is my strength and my song; he also is become my salvation.   Isaiah 12:1

I love them that love me; and those that seek me early shall find me.   Proverbs 8:17

Thou will keep him in perfect peace, whose mind is stayed on you, because he trusts in you. Isaiah 26:3

You have loved righteousness and hated iniquity, therefore God, even thy God hath anointed you, with the oil of gladness above thy fellows.

Hebrews 1:9

For it is written, as I live, says the Lord, every knee shall bow to me, and every tongue shall confess to

God; so then every one of us shall give account of himself to God.   Romans 14:11-12

In the beginning was the Word, and the Word was with God, and the Word was God.   John 1:1

Let the word of Christ dwell in you richly in all wisdom; teaching and admonishing one another in psalms and hymns and spiritual songs, singing with grace in your hearts to the Lord.   Colossians 3:16

PRAYER OF JABEZ

And Jabez called on the God of Israel saying, "Oh, that you would bless me indeed, and enlarge my territory, that your hand would be with me, and that you would keep *me* from evil, that I will be free from pain!" So God granted him that which he requested.   1 Chronicles 4:10

PRAYERS AND DECLARATIONS

Dear God, show us, teach us the knowledge of your ways. Job 21:14

So shall they fear the name of the Lord from the west, and his glory from the rising of the sun. When the enemy shall come in like a flood, the Spirit of the Lord shall lift up a standard against him. Isaiah 59:19

PRAY

Heavenly Father, let your holy fire consume all that is unholy in me. Let me know you as the God that dwells in the fire, to melt down and purge out and destroy what is not of you; to save and take up into your own holiness what is your own.

SPEAK YOUR DECLARATION

Heavenly Father, let us not love in word, neither in tongue; but in deed and in truth. 1 John 3:18

Father God, In the name of Jesus, I pray that the eyes of my spirit will be opened and enlightened as I read your word. I pray for a better understanding of God and His word. Saturate (soak) me with your word. Lord, may your word come alive in my heart. Help me to destroy quickly everything from Satan and meditate on your word day and night.

SPEAK YOUR DECLARATION

I pray that the Lord our God will show us the way wherein we may walk and the thing that we may do.

Jeremiah 42:3

PRAY

Holy God, please make us sensitive to the opportunities you bring our way, so that we will know, it is your open door.

Heavenly Father, I pray that your light will penetrate my whole being- spirit, mind and body. I command all darkness to leave; and I receive your power and holy light into every area of my life.

Father God, please give me a greater understanding of your word, a greater anointing to pray and a greater anointing to fast. Search my mind. Lord, do I have any double mindedness; I want to cut that out. Lord, is my spirit really pure before you? Have I confused or deceived myself in any way? Do I have any unbelief in my spirit?

SPEAK YOUR DECLARATION

Do not be anxious about anything, but in every situation, by prayer and supplication with thanksgiving let your requests be made known unto God. And the peace of God, which passes all understanding, shall keep your hearts and minds through Christ Jesus.   Philippians 4:6-7

Be not deceived, evil communications corrupt good manners.   1 Corinthians 15:33

Praise the Lord! For it is good to sing praises to our God; for it is pleasant, and praise is comely.
Psalm 147:1

PRAY

Holy God, please wash my steps with butter, and let the rock pour me out rivers of oil. Clothe me with righteousness and let my judgment be as a robe and a diadem. Help me to be eyes to the blind and feet to the lame. Help me to extend my hands to the poor and give me a sound mind that I may search out the cause which I know not. God, please spread my roots out by the water and let the dew lay all night upon my branch. Job 29:6

SPEAK YOUR DECLARATION

Finally, brethren, whatsoever things are true, whatsoever things are honest, whatsoever things are just, whatsoever things are pure, whatsoever things are lovely, whatsoever things are of good report; if there be any virtue, and if there be any praise, think on these things. Philippians 4:8

Call unto me and I will answer you, and show you great and mighty things, which you know not.
Jeremiah 33:3

PRAY

Heavenly Father, we give unto you praise, and honor, glory and thanksgiving. We worship you in the beauty of holiness. Lord your voice is powerful and full of majesty. You are King of Kings and Lord of Lords and sit as King forever. Lord, please fill our hearts and our homes with your spirit and make us aware of your holy presence.

SPEAK YOUR DECLARATION

As for me this is my covenant with you, says the Lord. My spirit that is upon you and my words that I have put in your mouth, shall not depart out of your mouth, nor out of the mouth of thy children or grandchildren or great-grandchildren, (any of your seed,) says the Lord, from henceforth and forever.

Isaiah 59:21

For God gives to a person that is good in His sight wisdom, and knowledge and joy; but to the sinner he gives travail, to gather and to heap up, that he may give to him that is good in his sight.

Ecclesiastes 2:26

For to be carnally (fleshly) minded is death; but to be spiritually minded is life and peace. Romans 8:6

SPEAK YOUR DECLARATION

Our praise, prayer and positive attitude releases God's presence, God's promises and God's power to work in our lives, giving us God's peace.

Oh that men would praise the Lord for his goodness, and for his wonderful works to the children of men.   Psalm 107:8

The Lord bless you more and more, you and your children; you are blessed of the Lord which made heaven and earth.   Psalm 115:14-15

OUR HERITAGE

Behold, children are a heritage from the Lord, The fruit of the womb is a reward. Like arrows in the hand of a warrior, so are the children of one's youth. Happy is the man who has his quiver full of them; they shall not be ashamed, but shall speak with their enemies in the gate.   Psalm 127:3-5

Train up a child in the way he should go: and when he is old, he will not depart from it.   Proverbs 22:6

Children, obey your parents in the Lord: for this is right. Ephesians 6:1

And you fathers, do not provoke your children to wrath, but bring them up in the training and admonition of the Lord. Ephesians 6:4

And these words which I command you today shall be in your heart. You shall teach them diligently to your children, and shall talk of them when you sit in your house, when you walk by the way, when you lie down, and when you rise up.

Deuteronomy 6: 6-7

All your children shall be taught by the LORD, and great shall be the peace of your children.

Isaiah 54:13

But you must continue in the things which you have learned and been assured of, knowing from whom you have learned them, and that from childhood you have known the Holy Scriptures, which are able to make you wise for salvation through faith which is in Christ Jesus. 2 Timothy 3:14-15

I can do all things through Christ which strengthens me. Philippians 4:13

Come, you children, listen to me; I will teach you the fear of the Lord. Psalm 34:11

I have no greater joy than to hear that my children are walking in the truth. 3 John 1:4

My son, be attentive to my words; incline you ear to my sayings. Let them not escape from your sight; keep them within your heart. For they are life to those who find them, and healing to all their flesh. Proverbs 4:20-22

Search me, God, and know my heart; test me and know my anxious thoughts. See if there is any offensive way in me, and lead me in the way everlasting. Psalm 139:23-24

Even a child is known by his deeds, whether what he does is pure and right. Proverbs 20:11

But Jesus said, "Suffer little children, and forbid them not, to come unto me: for of such is the kingdom of heaven." And he laid his hands on them and departed thence. Matthew 19:14

Children's children are the crown of old men; and the glory of children are their fathers.

Proverbs 17:6

PRAY FOR OUR LEGACY

Prayer releases the power of God to work in our lives; when we pray Gods Holy, Healing Spirit, flows through us.

I will pour my spirit on your descendants and my blessings on your offspring. All the power of hell cannot come close to withstanding the Holy Spirit poured out on your children's lives in response to your prayers.

Isaiah 44:3

But my servant Caleb, because he has a different spirit in him and has followed me fully, I will bring into the land where he went, and his descendants shall inherit it.

Numbers 14:24

O Lord, you are my God; I will exalt you, I will praise your name; for you have done wonderful things; your counsels of old are faithfulness and truth.   Isaiah: 25:1

O Lord, you have searched me and know me, you know when I sit down, and when I rise up, and you perceive my thoughts from afar. You discern my going out and my lying down; you are familiar with all my ways.   Psalm 139:1-3

For you created my inmost being; you knit me together in my mother's womb. I praise you because I am fearfully and wonderfully made; your works are wonderful; I know that full well. My frame was not hidden from you when I was made in the secret place, when I was woven together in the depths of the earth.   Psalm 139:13-15

Your eyes saw my unformed body; all the days ordained for me were written in your book before one of them came to be. How precious to me are your thoughts, God! How vast is the sum of them! Were I to count them, they would outnumber the grains of sand— when I awake, I am still with you.
                                                Psalm 139:16-18

Bless the Lord, O my soul and all that is within me, bless his holy name. Bless the Lord, O my soul, and forget not all his benefits.   Psalm 103:1-2

Help me to pray without ceasing and in everything give thanks for this is the will of God in Christ Jesus. Help me to rejoice evermore, quench not the spirit, despise not prophesying, prove all things, hold fast that which is good; Help me abstain from all appearance of evil. Father God, help me to die out to self and walk the straight and narrow way. Help me to be willing to be broken for you.

But seek first the kingdom of God, and his righteousness, and all these things shall be added to you.   Matthew 6:33

Heavenly Father, keep me aware that this is the day you have made and help me rejoice and be glad in it. Set a watch before my lips O Lord, and help me to understand the fear of the Lord and find the knowledge of God for he lays up sound wisdom for me; for he is a buckler unto them that walk uprightly.

And we have known and believed the love that God has for us. God is love; and he that dwells in love dwells in God, and God in him.

1 John 4:16

For God so loved the world, that he gave his only begotten Son, that whosoever believes in him should not perish, but have everlasting life.

John 3:16

PRAY

Father God, help me attend to your word and incline my ears to your sayings. Let your word depart not from my eyes; help me to keep them in the midst of my heart for they are life unto all flesh.

Help me to take hold of instruction, help me to keep her and not let her go- for she is life.

Lord God may my mouth speak wisdom and the meditation of my heart be understanding. Help me to absorb your word, let it linger deeply; impress it on my mind. Help me to pray without ceasing and in everything give thanks, for this is the will of God in Christ Jesus.

He said unto me, my grace is sufficient for you: for my strength is made perfect in weakness.

2 Corinthians: 12:9

Behold, I have graven you upon the palms of my hands; thy walls are continually before me.

Isaiah 49:16

No temptation has overtaken you except such as is common to man; but God is faithful, who will not allow you to be tempted beyond what you are able, but with the temptation will also make the way of escape, that you may be able to bear it.

1 Corinthians 10:13

THE WHOLE ARMOR OF GOD

Full Spiritual Battle Dress by Faith

Finally, my brethren, be strong in the Lord and in the power of His might. Put on the whole armor of God, that you may be able to stand against the wiles of the devil. For we do not wrestle against flesh and blood, but against principalities, against powers, against the rulers of the darkness of this world, against spiritual wickedness in high places. Therefore take up the whole armor of God that you may be able to withstand in the evil day, and having done all, to stand. Ephesians 6:10-13

Stand therefore, having girded your waist with truth, having put on the breastplate of righteousness, and having shod your feet with the preparation of the gospel of peace; above all, taking the shield of faith with which you will be able to quench all the fiery darts of the wicked. And take the helmet of salvation, and the sword of the Spirit, which is the word of God; praying always with all prayer and supplication in the Spirit, being watchful to this end with all perseverance and supplication for all the saints and for me, that utterance may be given to me, that I may open my mouth boldly to make known the mystery of the gospel, for which I

am an ambassador in bonds; that I may speak boldly, as I ought to speak.   Ephesians 6:14-20

BLESSINGS FOR OBEDIENCE

This book of the law shall not depart out of your mouth; but you shall meditate therein day and night, that you may observe to do according to all that is written therein: for then you shall make your way prosperous, and then you shall have good success.

Joshua 1:8

Thus says the Lord, your Redeemer, and The Holy One of Israel: "I am the Lord your God, who teaches you to profit, who leads you by the way you should go. Isaiah 48:17

I pray that you may be filled with the knowledge of God's will in all wisdom and spiritual understanding; that you may walk worthy of the Lord, fully pleasing him, being fruitful in every good work and increasing in the knowledge of God; strengthened with all might, according to his glorious power, for all patience and longsuffering with joy; giving thanks to the Father who has qualified us to be partakers of the inheritance of the saints in the light. Colossians 1:9-12

And let us not be weary in well doing: for in due season we shall reap, if we faint not.　　Galatians 6:9

Who hath delivered us from the power of darkness, and hath translated us into the kingdom of his dear Son; In whom we have redemption through his blood, even the forgiveness of sins; Who is the image of the invisible God, the firstborn of every creature:　　Colossians 1:13-15

So then faith comes by hearing, and hearing by the word of God.　　Romans 10:17

Fear not, for I am with you; be not dismayed, for I am your God.　I will strengthen you, Yes, I will help you, I will uphold you with my righteous right hand.　　Isaiah 41:10

Blessed be God, even the Father of our Lord Jesus Christ, the Father of mercies, and the God of all comfort; Who comforts us in all our tribulation, that we may be able to comfort them which are in any trouble,　by the comfort wherewith we ourselves are comforted of God.　　2 Corinthians 1:3-4

Praise the Lord; I will praise the Lord with my whole heart, in the assembly of the upright, and in the congregation.   Psalm 111:1

Now may the God of hope fill you with all joy and peace in believing, that you may abound in hope by the power of the Holy Spirit.   Romans 15:13

I pray that the God of our Lord Jesus Christ, the Father of glory, may give you the spirit of wisdom and revelation in the knowledge of him. The eyes of your understanding being enlightened; that you may know what is the hope of his calling, what are the riches of the glory of his inheritance in the saints, and what is the exceeding greatness of his power toward us who believe, according to the working of his mighty power which he worked in Christ when he raised him from the dead and seated him at his right hand in the heavenly places; far above all principality and power and might and dominion, and every name that is named not only in this age but also in that which is to come.

                    Ephesians 1:17-21

I pray that God would grant you, according to the riches of his glory, to be strengthened with might through his Spirit in the inner man, that Christ may dwell in your hearts through faith; that you, being rooted and grounded in love, may be able to comprehend with all the saints what is the width and length and depth and height- to know the love of Christ which passes knowledge; that you may be filled with all the fullness of God.

Ephesians 3:16-19

But you are a chosen generation, a royal priesthood, a holy nation, His special people, that you should show forth the praises of him who called you out of darkness into his marvelous light.   1 Peter 2:9

And this I pray, that your love may abound still more and more in knowledge and all discernment; that you may approve the things that are excellent, that you may be sincere and without offense till the day of Christ, being filled with the fruits of righteousness which are by Jesus Christ, to the glory and praise of God.   Philippians 1:9-11

Do all things without murmurings and disputing; that you may be blameless and harmless, the sons of

God, without rebuke, in the midst of a crooked and perverse nation, among whom you shine as lights in the world. Philippians 2:14-15

Let the word of Christ dwell in you richly in all wisdom, teaching and admonishing one another in psalms and hymns and spiritual songs, singing with grace in your hearts to the Lord. Colossians 3:16

For verily I say unto you, that whosoever shall say unto this mountain, Be thou removed, and be thou cast, into the sea; and shall not doubt in his heart, but shall believe that those things which he says shall come to pass; he shall have whatsoever he says. Mark 11:23

Blessed is the person that hears me, watching daily at my gates, waiting at the posts of my doors.
Proverbs 8:34

And Jesus said unto them, "Because you have so little faith, truly I tell you, if you have faith as small as a mustard seed, you can say to this mountain, "Move from here to there," and it will move. Nothing will be impossible for you."
Matthew 17:20

For God so loved the world, that he gave his only begotten Son, that whosoever believes in him should not perish, but have everlasting life.

John 3:16

And Jesus said, "The things which are impossible with men are possible with God."   Luke 18:27

"Let us therefore come boldly unto the throne of grace, that we may obtain mercy, and find grace to help in time of need."   Hebrews 4:16

"For God hath not given us the spirit of fear; but of power, and of love, and of a sound mind."

2 Timothy 1:7

And we know that all things work together for good to them that love God, to them who are called according to his purpose.   Romans 8:28

They that wait upon the Lord shall renew their strength; they shall mount up with wings as eagles; they shall run, and not be weary; and they shall walk, and not faint.   Isaiah 40:31

I waited patiently for the Lord; and he inclined unto me and heard my cry. He brought me up also out of a horrible pit, out of the miry clay, and set my feet upon a rock, and established my goings. And he has put a new song in my mouth, even praise unto our God; many shall see it, and fear, and shall trust in the Lord. Blessed is that man that makes the Lord his trust, and respects not the proud, nor such as turn aside to lies. Psalm 40:1-4

Wait on the Lord: be of good courage, and he will strengthen your heart: wait, I say, on the Lord. Psalm 27:14

The Lord will perfect that which concerns me: thy mercy, O Lord, endures for ever: forsake not the works of your own hands. Psalm 138:8

For we have not an high priest which cannot be touched with the feelings of our infirmities; but was in all points tempted like as we are, yet without sin. Let us therefore come boldly unto the throne of grace, that we may obtain mercy, and find grace to help in time of need. Hebrews 4:15-16

And this is the confidence that we have in him, that if we ask any thing according to his will, he hears us: And if we know that he hear us, whatsoever we ask, we know that we have the petitions that we desired of him. 1 John 5:14-15

I will lift up my eyes unto the hills, from whence comes my help. My help comes from the Lord which made heaven and earth. Psalm 121:1-2

He was wounded for our transgressions; he was bruised for our iniquities: the chastisement of our peace was upon him; and with his stripes we are healed. Isaiah 53:5

By him therefore let us offer the sacrifice of praise to God continually, that is, the fruit of our lips giving thanks to his name. Hebrews 13:15

Beloved, I pray above all things that you may prosper and be in health, even as your soul prospers. 3 John:2

Because your loving kindness is better than life, my lips shall praise you. Thus will I bless you while I live: I will lift up my hands in your name. My soul shall be satisfied as with marrow and fatness; and my mouth shall praise you with joyful lips.

Psalms 63:3-5

It is a good thing to give thanks unto the Lord, and to sing praises unto your name, O Most High: To show forth your loving kindness in the morning, and your faithfulness every night.   Psalm 92:1-2

For the Lord is great, and greatly to be praised: he is to be feared (respected) above all gods. Psalms 96:4

Make a joyful noise unto the Lord, all you lands. Serve the Lord with gladness: come before his presence with singing. Know you that the Lord he is God: it is he that has made us, and not we ourselves; we are his people, and the sheep of his pasture. Enter into his gates with thanksgiving, and into his courts with praise: be thankful unto him, and bless his name. For the Lord is good; his mercy is everlasting; and his truth endures to all generations.   Psalm 100

For the scripture says, whosoever believes on him shall not be ashamed.   Romans 10:11

Trust in the Lord with all your heart; and lean not on your own understanding.   In all your ways acknowledge him, and he shall direct your paths.

Proverbs 3:5-6

The Lord takes pleasure in them that fear him, in those that hope in his mercy.   Psalm 147:11

But you, O Lord, are a shield for me; my glory, and the lifter up of my head. I cried unto the Lord with my voice, and he heard me out of his holy hill.

Psalm 3:3-4

Your word have I hid in my heart, that I might not sin against you. Blessed art thou, O Lord: teach me your statutes.   Psalm 119:11-12

At *midnight* I will rise to give thanks unto you because of your righteous judgments. Psalm 119:62

And at *midnight* Paul and Silas prayed, and sang praises unto God: and the prisoners heard them.

Acts 16:25

Your word is a lamp unto my feet, and a light unto my path. Psalm 119:105

Now abides faith, hope and love, these three; but the greatest of these is love. 1 Corinthians 13:13

Every word of God is pure: he is a shield unto them that put their trust in him. Proverbs 30:5

Have you not known? Have you not heard? The everlasting God, the Lord, the Creator of the ends of the earth, neither faints nor is weary. His understanding is unsearchable. He gives power to the weak, and to those who have no might He increases strength. Isaiah 40:28-29

They that wait upon the Lord shall renew their strength; they shall mount up with wings as eagles; they shall run, and not be weary; and they shall walk, and not faint. Isaiah 40:31

Therefore, if any man be in Christ, he is a new creature: old things are passed away; all things are become new. 2 Corinthians 5:17

The Lord is my strength and my shield, my heart trusts in him and I am helped; with my song will I praise him.   God is our strength and the saving strength of his anointed.   Psalm 28:7

Behold, I set before you this day a blessing and a curse; A blessing, if you obey the commandments of the Lord your God, which I command you this day: And a curse, if you will not obey the commandments of the Lord your God, but turn aside out of the way which I command you this day, to go after other gods, which you have not known.
Deuteronomy 11:26-28

LOVE

Though I speak with the tongues of men and of angels, and have not love, I am become as sounding brass, or a tinkling cymbal. And though I have the gift of prophecy, and understand all mysteries, and all knowledge; and though I have all faith, so that I could remove mountains, and have not love, I am nothing. And though I bestow all my goods to feed the poor, and though I give my body to be burned, and have not love, it profits me nothing.

1 Corinthians 13:1-3

Love suffers long, and is kind; love envies not; love vaunts not itself, is not puffed up; Does not behave itself unseemly, seeks not her own, is not easily provoked, thinks no evil; rejoices not in iniquity, but rejoices in the truth; bears all things, believes all things, hopes all things, endures all things. Love never fails: but whether there be prophecies, they shall fail; whether there be tongues, they shall cease; whether there be knowledge, it shall vanish away. And now abides faith, hope, and love, these three; but the greatest of these is love: Corinthians 13:4-8:13

Now faith is the substance of things hoped for, the evidence of things not seen. Hebrews 11:1

For we walk by faith, not by sight. 2 Corinthians 5:7

For as the body without the spirit is dead, so faith without works is dead. James 2:26

Through faith we understand that the worlds were framed by the word of God, so that things which are seen were not made of things which do appear.

Hebrews 11:3

But let him ask in faith, nothing wavering. For he that wavers is like a wave of the sea driven with the wind and tossed. James 1:6

HEALING PRAYERS

And Jesus said unto him, "Go your way; your faith has made you whole." And immediately he received his sight, and followed Jesus in the way.

Mark 10:52

And, behold, a woman, which was diseased with an issue of blood twelve years, came behind him, and touched the hem of his garment: For she said within herself, If I may but touch his garment, I shall be whole. But Jesus turned him about, and when he saw her, he said, Daughter, be of good comfort; thy faith hath made thee whole. And the woman was made whole from that hour.

Matthew 9:20-22

Is any sick among you? Let him call for the elders of the church; and let them pray over him, anointing him with oil in the name of the Lord: And the prayer of faith shall save the sick, and the Lord shall raise him up; and if he have committed sins, they shall be forgiven him.

James 5:14-15

You will keep him in perfect peace, whose mind is stayed on you: because he trusts in you. Isaiah 26:3

The centurion answered and said, Lord, I am not worthy that you should come under my roof: but speak the word only, and my servant shall be healed.   Matthew 8:8

Did not we cast three men bound into the midst of the fire? He (Nebuchadnezzar) answered and said, Lo, I see four men loose, walking in the midst of the fire, and they have no hurt; and the form of the fourth is like the Son of God.   Daniel 3:24-25

If you then, being evil, know how to give good gifts unto your children: how much more shall your heavenly Father give the Holy Spirit to them that ask him?   Luke 11:13

If you claim to be religious but don't control your tongue, you are fooling yourself, and your religion is worthless.   James 1:26

And they said, Believe on the Lord Jesus Christ, and you shall be saved, and your house. Acts 16:31

Knowing that a man is not justified by the works of the law, but by the faith of Jesus Christ, even we have believed in Jesus Christ, that we might be justified by the faith of Christ, and not by the works of the law: for by the works of the law shall no flesh be justified. Galatians 2:16

But you, when you pray, enter into your closet, and when you have shut your door, pray to your Father which is in secret; and your Father which sees in secret shall reward you openly. Matthew 6:6

And Jesus answering said unto him, have faith in God. Mark 11:22

O God, you have taught me from my youth: and hitherto have I declared your wondrous works. Now also when I am old and grey headed, O God, forsake me not; until I have showed your strength unto this generation, and your power to everyone that is to come. Psalm 71:17-18

But grow in grace, and in the knowledge of our Lord and Savior Jesus Christ. To him be glory both now and forever. Amen 2 Peter 3:18

For the word of God is quick, and powerful, and sharper than any two- edged sword, piercing even to the dividing asunder of soul and spirit, and of the joints and marrow, and is a discerner of the thoughts and intents of the heart.   Hebrews 4:12

And whatsoever you do, do it heartily, as to the Lord, and not unto men; knowing that of the Lord you shall receive the reward of the inheritance: for you serve the Lord Christ.   Colossians 3:23-24

He restores my soul: he leads me in the paths of righteousness for his name's sake.   Psalm 23:3

The Lord is my light and my salvation; whom shall I fear? The Lord is the strength of my life; of whom shall I be afraid?   Psalm 27:1

One thing have I desired of the Lord, that will I seek after; that I may dwell in the house of the Lord all the days of my life, to behold the beauty of the Lord, and to inquire in his temple.   Psalm 27:4

If any of you lacks wisdom, you should ask God, who gives generously to all without reproach; and it shall be given to you.   James 1:5

I will exalt you, O Lord, for you have lifted me up, and have not let my enemies rejoice over me. O Lord my God, I cried out to you, and you healed me. You have kept me alive, that I should not go down to the pit. Sing praise to the Lord, you saints of his, and give thanks at the remembrance of his holy name. For his anger is but for a moment, his favor is for life; weeping may endure for a night, but joy comes in the morning.   Psalm 30:1-5

Trust in the Lord with all your heart; and lean not on your own understanding; in all your ways acknowledge him, and he will direct your paths.

Proverbs 3:5-6

Wait on the Lord: be of good courage, and he shall strengthen your heart: wait, I say, on the Lord.

Psalm 27:14

When you lie down, you shall not be afraid: yes, you shall lie down, and your sleep shall be sweet.

Proverbs 3:24

I will both lay me down in peace, and sleep: for thou, Lord, only make me dwell in safety. Psalm 4:8

Blessed is the man who endures temptation; for when he has been approved, he will receive the crown of life which the Lord has promised to those who love him.   James 1:12

He that dwells in the secret place of the most high shall abide under the shadow of the Almighty. I will say of the Lord, He is my refuge and my fortress: my God; in him will I trust.   Psalm 91:1-2

Let the wicked forsake his way, and the unrighteous man his thoughts: and let him return unto the Lord, and he will have mercy upon him; and to our God, for he will abundantly pardon.   Isaiah 55:7

Be careful for nothing; but in everything by prayer and supplication with thanksgiving let your requests be made known unto God. And the peace of God, which passes all understanding, shall keep your hearts and minds through Christ Jesus.

Philippians 4:6-7

Watch and pray that you may not enter into temptation. The spirit indeed is willing, but the flesh is weak.   Matthew 26:41

Submit yourselves therefore to God. Resist the devil, and he will flee from you. Draw near to God, and he will draw near to you. Cleanse your hands, you sinners; and purify your hearts, you double minded.   James 4:7-8

For if you forgive men their trespasses, your heavenly Father will also forgive you. But if you forgive not men their trespasses, neither will your Father forgive your trespasses.   Matthew 6:14-15

If we confess our sins, he is faithful and just to forgive us our sins, and to cleanse us from all unrighteousness.   1 John 1:9

For you were sometimes darkness, but now are you light in the Lord: walk as children of light.

Ephesians 5:8

Even though Jesus was God's Son, he learned obedience from the things which he suffered.

Hebrews 5:8

Do not merely listen to the word, and so deceive yourselves, Do what it says.   James 1:22

Therefore, my dear brothers and sisters, stand firm. Let nothing move you. Always give yourselves fully to the work of the Lord, because you know that your labor in the Lord is not in vain.

1 Corinthians 15:58

Bless the Lord, O my soul and all that is within me, bless His holy name. Bless the Lord, O my soul, and forget not all His benefits.   Psalm 103:1-2

Hereby we know the spirit of truth, and the spirit of error. Beloved, let us love one another: for love is of God; and everyone that loves is born of God, and knows God. He that loves not knows not God; for God is love.   1 John 4:7-8

If my people, who are called by my name, will humble themselves and pray and seek my face and turn from their wicked ways, then I will hear from heaven, and I will forgive their sin and will heal their land.   2 Chronicles 7:14

You are the light of the world. A city that is set on a hill cannot be hidden. Nor do they light a lamp and put it under a basket, but on a lamp stand, and it gives light to all who are in the house. Let your light so shine before men, that they may see your good works and glorify your Father in heaven.

Matthew 5:14-16

The Lord is nigh unto all them that call upon him, to all that call upon him in truth.   Psalms 145:18

I will therefore that men pray everywhere, lifting up holy hands without wrath and doubting.

1Timothy 2:8

Seek the Lord while he may be found; call on him while he is near.   Isaiah 55:61

No matter how softly you whisper a prayer,
God hears and understands.
He knows the hopes and fears you keep in your
heart; when you trust Him miracles happen.
(copied)

And whatever you ask in my name, that I will do, that the Father may be glorified in the Son. If you ask anything in my name, I will do it. John 14:13-14

In the same way, the Spirit helps us in our weakness. We do not know what we ought to pray for, but the Sprit himself intercedes for us through wordless groans. Romans 8:26

Now unto him that is able to do exceeding abundantly above all that we ask or think, according to the power that works in us, unto him be glory in the church by Christ Jesus throughout all ages, world without end. Ephesians 3:20

Let us therefore come boldly unto the throne of grace, that we may obtain mercy, and find grace to help in time of need. Hebrews 4:16

Your word have I hid in my heart, that I might not sin against you. Blessed art thou, O Lord: teach me your statutes. Psalm 119:11-12

FAITH

And without faith it is impossible to please God, because anyone who comes to him must believe that he exists and that he rewards those who earnestly seek him.   Hebrews 11:6

If you remain in me and my words remain in you, ask whatever you wish, and it will be done for you.   John 15:7

Elijah was a human being, even as we are. He prayed earnestly that it would not rain, and it did not rain on the land for three and a half years. Again he prayed, and the heavens gave rain, and the earth produced its crops.   James 5:17-18

Cast your burden upon the Lord, and he shall sustain thee: he will never suffer the righteous to be moved.   Psalm 55:22

And now, brethren, I commend you to God, and to the word of his grace, which is able to build you up, and to give you an inheritance among all them which are sanctified.   Acts 20:32

Commit to the Lord whatever you do, and he will establish your plans.   Proverbs 16:3

But as it is written, Eye hath not seen, nor ear heard, neither have entered into the heart of man, the things which God hath prepared for them that love him.   1 Corinthians 2:9

Bless the Lord, O my soul, and forget not all his benefits: who forgives all your iniquities; who heals all your diseases; who redeems your life from destruction; who crowns you with loving kindness and tender mercies; who satisfies your soul with good things; so that your youth is renewed like the eagle's.   Psalm 103:2-5

But as God has distributed to every man, as the Lord has called every one, so let him walk.
                               1 Corinthians 7:17

Let your conversation be without covetousness; and be content with such things as you have, for he has said, I will never leave you, nor forsake you.
                               Hebrews 13:5

Blessed are they which do hunger and thirst after righteousness; for they shall be filled. Matthew 5:6

And you shall love the Lord your God with all your heart, and with all your soul, and with all your might.   Deuteronomy 6:5

The Lord bless you and keep you; the Lord make his face shine upon you and be gracious to you; the Lord lift up his countenance upon you and give you peace.   Numbers 6:24-26

For I know the plans I have for you, declares the Lord, plans to prosper you and not to harm you, plans to give you a hope and a future. Jeremiah 29:11

Come to me, all you who are weary and burdened, and I will give you rest. Take my yoke upon you and learn from me, for I am gentle and humble in heart, and you will find rest for your souls, for my yoke is easy and my burden is light.

Matthew 11:28-30

The good person out of the good treasure of his heart produces good, and the evil person out of his evil treasure produces evil, for out of the abundance of the heart his mouth speaks.   Luke 6:45

Blessed be the God and Father of our Lord Jesus Christ, who has blessed us in Christ with every spiritual blessing in the heavenly places, even as he chose us in him before the foundation of the world, that we should be holy and blameless before him.

Ephesians 1:3-4

Blessed is the man who walks not in the counsel of the wicked, nor stands in the way of sinners, nor sits in the seat of scoffers; but his delight is in the law of the Lord, and on his law he meditates day and night. He is like a tree planted by streams of water that yields its fruit in its season and its leaf does not wither. In all that he does, he prospers. Psalm 1:1-3

But to all who did receive him, who believed in his name, he gave the right to become children of God, who were born, not of blood, nor of the will of the flesh, nor of the will of man, but of God.

John 1:12-13

And it shall come to pass that everyone who calls upon the name of the Lord shall be saved. Acts 2:21

The Lord will cause your enemies who rise against you to be defeated before you. They shall come out against you one way and flee before you seven ways.   Deuteronomy 28:7

THE LORD'S MODEL PRAYER

In this manner, therefore, pray:

Our Father in heaven, Hallowed be your name, your kingdom come, your will be done, on earth as it is in heaven. Give us this day our daily bread, and forgive us our debts, as we forgive our debtors. And do not lead us into temptation, but deliver us from the evil one. For yours is the kingdom and the power and the glory forever. Amen Matthew 6:9-13

THE FRUIT OF THE SPIRIT

But the fruit of the Spirit is love, joy, peace, longsuffering, kindness, goodness, faithfulness, gentleness, self-control. Against such there is no law. Galatians 5:22-23

For there is not a just man upon earth, that does good, and sins not. Ecclesiastes: 7:20

I am the vine, you are the branches. He who abides in me, and I in him, bears much fruit; for without me you can do nothing. John 15:5

Ask, and it shall be given you; seek, and you shall find; knock and it shall be opened unto you: For every one that asks receives; and he that seeks finds; and to him that knocks it shall be opened.
Matthew 7:7-8

Blessed are the peacemakers, for they shall be called sons of God. Matthew 5:9

It will also come to pass, that before they call I will answer; and while they are still speaking, I will hear. Isaiah 65:24

THE SHEPHERD'S VIEW POINT

The Lord is my shepherd; I shall not want. He makes me to lie down in green pastures; He leads me beside the still waters. He restores my soul; He leads me in the paths of righteousness for his name's sake. Yea, though I walk through the valley of the shadow of death, I will fear no evil; for you are with me; your rod and your staff, they comfort me. You prepare a table before me in the presence of my enemies; you anoint my head with oil; my cup runs over. Surely goodness and mercy shall follow me all the days of my life, and I will dwell in the house of the Lord forever.   Psalm 23

Jesus answered, "I am the way and the truth and the life. No one comes to the father except through me."   John 14:6

The name of the Lord is a strong tower: the righteous run into it, and is safe.   Proverbs 18:10

Be strong and of a good courage, fear not, nor be afraid of them: for the Lord your God, he it is that goes with you; he will not fail you, nor forsake you.

Deuteronomy 31:6

Let us hear the conclusion of the whole matter: Fear God and keep his commandments; for this is the whole duty of man. For God shall bring every work into judgment, with every secret thing, whether it be good, or whether it be evil.   Ecclesiastes 12:13-14

I will sing of the mercies of the Lord forever; with my mouth will I make known your faithfulness to all generations. For I have said, "Mercy shall be built up forever; your faithfulness you shall establish in the very heavens." Nevertheless, my loving kindness I will not utterly take from him, nor allow my faithfulness to fail. My covenant I will not break, nor alter the word that has gone out of my lips.   Psalm 89:1-2-33-34

Through him then let us continually offer up a sacrifice of praise to God, that is, the fruit of lips that acknowledge his name.   Hebrews 13:15

Let the word of Christ dwell in you richly, teaching and admonishing one another in all wisdom, singing psalms and hymns and spiritual songs, with thankfulness in your hearts to God.

Colossians 3:16

Praise the Lord, all nations! Exalt him, all people; for great is his steadfast love toward us, and the faithfulness of the Lord endures forever. Praise the Lord! Psalm 117:1-2

Speaking to yourselves in psalms and hymns and spiritual songs, singing and making melody in your heart to the Lord. Ephesians 5:19

The Lord your God is in your midst, a mighty one who will save; he will rejoice over you with gladness; he will quiet you by his love; he will exalt over you with loud singing. Zephaniah 3:17

You have turned for me my mourning into dancing; you have loosed my sackcloth and clothed me with gladness. Psalm 30:11

Oh come, let us worship and bow down; let us kneel before the Lord, our Maker! Psalm 95:6

Truly my soul silently waits for God, from him comes my salvation. He only is my rock and my salvation; he is my defense; I shall not be greatly moved. How long will you attack a man? You shall be slain, all of you, like a leaning wall and a tottering fence. They only consult to cast him down from his high position; they delight in lies; they bless with their mouth, but they curse inwardly. My Soul, wait silently for God alone, for my expectation is from him. Psalm 62:1-5

So continuing daily with one accord in the temple, and breaking bread from house to house, they ate their food with gladness and simplicity of heart, praising God and having favor with all the people. And the Lord added to the church daily those who were being saved. Acts 2: 46-47

Out of the same mouth proceed blessing and cursing. My brethren, these things ought not to be so. James 3:10

Heal me, O Lord, and I shall be healed; Save me, and I shall be saved, for you are my praise.

Jeremiah 17:14

BE ALERT

Beloved, do not believe every spirit, but test the spirits, whether they are of God; because many false prophets have gone out into the world. By this you know the Spirit of God: Every spirit that confesses that Jesus Christ has come in the flesh is of God, and every spirit that does not confess that Jesus Christ has come in the flesh is not of God. And this is the spirit of antichrist, which you have heard was coming, and is now already in the world. You are of God, little children, and have overcome them, because he who is in you is greater than he who is in the world.   1 John 4:1-4

Who hath delivered us from the power of darkness, and hath translated us into the kingdom of his dear Son: In whom we have redemption through his blood, even the forgiveness of sins:

Colossians 1:13-14

Be sober, be vigilant; because your adversary the devil, as a roaring lion, walks about, seeking whom he may devour: Whom resist steadfast in the faith, knowing that the same afflictions are accomplished in your brethren that are in the world.

1Peter 5:8-9

Submit yourselves therefore to God, resist the devil, and he will flee from you.

James 4:7

Therefore if any man be in Christ, he is a new creature: old things are passed away; behold all things are become new.

2 Corinthians 5:17

Who hath saved us, and called us with a holy calling, not according to our works, but according to his own purpose and grace, which was given us in Christ Jesus before the world began.

2 Timothy 1:9

That if you shall confess with your mouth the Lord Jesus, and shall believe in your heart that God has raised him from the dead, you shall be saved. For with the heart man believes unto righteousness; and with the mouth confession is made unto salvation.

Romans 10:9-10

Neither yield your members as instruments of unrighteousness unto sin: but yield yourselves unto God, as those that are alive from the dead, and your members as instruments of righteousness unto God; for sin shall not have dominion over you for you are not under the law, but under grace. What then? Shall we sin, because we are not under the law, but under grace? God forbid. Know you not, that to whom you yield yourselves servants to obey, his servants you are to whom you obey; whether of sin unto death, or of obedience unto righteousness?

Romans 6:14-16

For though we walk in the flesh, we do not war after the flesh: (For the weapons of our warfare not carnal, but mighty through God to the pulling down of strong holds;) Casting down imaginations, and every high thing that exalts itself against the knowledge of God, and bringing into captivity every thought to the obedience of Christ.

2 Corinthians 10:3-5

He that commits sin is of the devil; for the devil sins from the beginning. For this purpose the Son of God was manifested, that he might destroy the works of the devil.

1 John 3:8

The name of the Lord is a strong tower: the righteous run to it and are safe.

Proverbs 18:10

And the God of peace shall bruise Satan under your feet shortly.   The grace of our Lord Jesus Christ be with you. Amen.   Romans 16:20

For whether we live, we live unto the Lord; and whether we die, we die unto the Lord: whether we live therefore, or die, we are the Lord's.

Romans 14:8

For the Lord God will help me: therefore shall I not be confounded: therefore have I set my face like a flint, and I know that I shall not be ashamed.

Isaiah 50:7

And there shall be signs in the sun, and in the moon, and in the stars; and upon the earth distress of nations with perplexity, the sea and the waves roaring. Men's hearts failing them for fear, and for looking after those things which are coming on the earth: for the powers of heaven shall be shaken. Then they shall see the Son of man coming in a cloud with power and great glory. And when these things begin to come to pass, then look up, and lift up your heads; for your redemption draws near.

Luke 21:25-28

Watch therefore, and pray always, that you may be accounted worthy to escape all these things that shall come to pass and to stand before the Son of man.

Luke 21:36

Know this also, that in the last days perilous times shall come. Men shall be lovers of their own selves, covetous, boasters, proud, blasphemers, disobedient to parents, unthankful, unholy, without natural affection, truce- breakers, false accusers, incontinent, fierce, despisers of those that are good, traitors, heady, high-minded, lovers of pleasures more than lovers of God; Having a form of godliness, but denying the power thereof; from such turn away.

2 Timothy 3:1-5

Prove all things; hold fast that which is good. Abstain from all appearance of evil.

1 Thessalonians 5:21-22

If we believe not, yet he abides faithful: he cannot deny himself. Nevertheless, the foundation of God stands sure, having this seal the Lord knows them that are his. And let everyone that names the name of Christ depart from iniquity.

2 Timothy 2:13, 19

The Lord is not slack concerning his promise, as some men count slackness; but is longsuffering to us-ward, not willing that any should perish, but that all should come to repentance.

2 Peter 3:9

He will not suffer your foot to be moved: he that keeps you will not slumber. Behold, he that keeps Israel shall neither slumber nor sleep.

Psalm 121:3-4

You shall lay up these my words in your heart and in your soul, and bind them for a sign upon your hand, that they may be as frontlets between your eyes. And you shall teach them to your children, speaking of them when you sit in your house, and when you walk by the way, when you lie down and when you rise up.

Deuteronomy 11:18-19

A man shall eat good by the fruit of his mouth: but the soul of the transgressors shall eat violence. He that keeps his mouth keeps his life: but he that opens wide his lips shall have destruction.

Proverbs 13:2-3

A good man out of the good treasure of the heart brings forth good things; and an evil man out of the evil treasure brings forth evil things. But I say unto you, that every idle word that men shall speak, they shall give account thereof in the day of judgment for by your words you shall be justified, and by your words you shall be condemned.

Matthew 12:35-37

And it shall come to pass, that before they call, I will answer; and while they are yet speaking, I will hear.

Isaiah 65:24

Again I say unto you, that if two of you shall agree on earth as touching anything that they shall ask, it shall be done for them of my Father which is in heaven. For where two or three are gathered together in my name, there am I in the midst of them.

Matthew 18:19-20

Therefore, I say unto you, What things so ever you desire, when you pray, believe that you receive them, and you shall have them.   Mark 11:24

But thou, when thou pray, enter into your closet, and when you have shut the door, pray to your Father which is in secret: and your Father which sees in secret shall reward you openly.
Matthew 6:6

The Lord is far from the wicked: but he hears the prayer of the righteous.   Proverbs 15:29

Delight yourself also in the Lord; and he shall give you the desires of your heart.   Psalm 37:4

The spirit of the Lord is upon me, because he hath anointed me to preach the gospel to the poor; he hath sent me to heal the broken hearted, to preach deliverance to the captives, and recovering of sight to the blind, to set at liberty them that are bruised, to preach the acceptable year of the Lord.
Luke 4:18-19

GOD LOVES YOU

Herein is our love made perfect, that we may have boldness in the day of judgment because as he is, so are we in this world. There is no fear in love; but perfect love casts out fear; because fear has torment. He that fears is not made perfect in love. We love him because he first loved us. If a man say, I love God and hates his brother, he is a liar: for he that loves not his brother whom he has seen, how can he love God whom he has not seen.   1 John 4:16-20

And you shall love the Lord your God with all your heart, and with all your soul, and with all your mind, and with all your strength; this is the first commandment.   And the second is this, you shall love your neighbor as thyself.   There is none other commandment greater than these.   And the scribe said unto him, Well, Master, thou hast said the truth: for there is one God; and there is none other but he: And to love him with all your heart, and with all your understanding, and with all your soul, and with all your strength and to love your neighbor as yourself, is more than all whole burnt offerings and sacrifices. Mark 12:30-33

The Lord hath appeared of old unto me, saying, I have loved you with an everlasting love: therefore with loving-kindness have I drawn you.

Jeremiah 31:3

And he arose, and rebuked the wind, and said unto the sea, Peace, be still. And the wind ceased, and there was a great calm. Mark 4:39

For I have not spoken of myself; but the Father which sent me, he gave me a commandment, what I should say, and I should speak. And I know that his commandment is life everlasting; whatsoever I speak therefore, even as the Father said unto me, so I speak. John 12:49-50

The wise in heart shall be called prudent; and the sweetness of the lips increases learning. Understanding is a wellspring of life unto him that has it; but the instruction of fools is folly. The heart of the wise teaches his mouth, and adds learning to his lips. Proverbs 16:21-23

Pleasant words are as an honeycomb, sweet to the soul, and health to the bones. There is a way that seems right unto a man, but the end thereof are the ways of death. He that labors, labors for himself; for his mouth craves it of him. An ungodly man digs up evil; and in his lips there is as a burning fire.

Proverbs 16:24-27

You shall know the truth, and the truth shall make you free. John 8:32

For the Son of man is come to seek and to save that which was lost. Luke 19:10

The words of a man's mouth are as deep waters, and the wellspring of wisdom as a flowing brook. A fool's mouth is his destruction, and his lips are the snare of his soul. The words of a talebearer are as wounds, and they go down into the innermost parts of the belly. A man's belly shall be satisfied with the fruit of his mouth: and with the increase of his lips shall he be filled. Death and life are in the power of the tongue; and they that love it shall eat the fruit thereof. Proverbs 18:4-6-7-8-20-21

For God sent not his Son into the world to condemn the world; but that the world through him might be saved.   John 3:17

FORGIVE

And when you stand praying, forgive, if you have aught against any; that your Father also which is in heaven may forgive you your trespasses.

Mark 11:25

For if you forgive men their trespasses, your heavenly Father will also forgive you, but if you forgive not men their trespasses, neither will your Father forgive your trespasses.

Matthew 6:14-15

For this is thankworthy if a man for conscience toward God endure grief, suffering wrongfully. For what glory is it, if you be buffeted for your faults, you shall take it patiently? But if, when you do well, and suffer for it, you take it patiently this is acceptable with God. For even here unto were you called; because Christ also suffered for us, leaving us an example, that you should follow his steps; who did no sin, neither was guile found in his mouth. Who when he was reviled, reviled not again; when he suffered, he threatened not; but committed himself to him that judge righteously.

1 Peter 2:19-20

But I say unto you, Love your enemies, bless them that curse you, do good to them that hate you, and pray for them which despitefully use you, and persecute you.   Matthew 5:44

Not rendering evil for evil, or railing for railing; but contrariwise blessing; knowing that you are there unto called, that you should inherit a blessing. For he that will love life, and see good days, let him refrain his tongue from evil, and his lips that they speak no guile.   1Peter 3:9-10

And he said unto them, Go ye into all the world, and preach the gospel to every creature.

Mark 16:15

Let all bitterness, and wrath, and anger, and clamor, and evil speaking, be put away from you, with all malice; And be kind one to another, tender-hearted, forgiving one another, even as God for Christ's sake has forgiven you.   Ephesians 4:31-32

And whosoever shall give to drink unto one of these little ones a cup of cold water only in the name of a disciple, verily I say unto you, he shall in no wise lose his reward.   Matthew 10:42

Set your mind on things above, not on things that are on earth, for you have died, and your life is hidden with Christ in God. When Christ who is your life appears, then you also will appear with him in glory.   Colossians 3:2-4

For we are his workmanship created in Christ Jesus for good works, which God prepared before hand, that we should walk in them.

Ephesians 2:10

Therefore, my beloved, as you have always obeyed, so now, not only as in my presence but much more in my absence. Work out your own salvation with fear and trembling, for it is God who works in you, both to will and to work for his good pleasure.

Philippians 2:12-13

You are the salt of the earth: but if the salt have lost his flavor, wherewith shall it be salted: it is therefore good for nothing, but to be cast out, and to be trodden under foot of men. You are the light of the world. A city that is set on a hill cannot be hid.

Neither do men light a candle, and put it under a bushel, but on a candle stick and it gives light unto all that are in the house. Let your light so shine before men, that they may see your good works, and glorify your Father which is in heaven.

Matthew 5:13-16

Pure religion and undefiled before God and the Father is this, to visit the fatherless and widows in their affliction, and to keep himself unspotted from the world.   James 1:27

When you go, they shall lead you; when you sleep, they shall keep you; and when you awake, they shall talk with you. For the commandment is a lamp; and the law is light; and reproofs of instruction are the way of life:

Proverbs 6:22-23

Trust in the Lord with all your heart, and lean not on your own understanding; in all your ways acknowledge him and he shall direct your paths. Do not be wise in your own eyes; fear the Lord and depart from evil; it will be health to your flesh, and strength to your bones.   Proverbs 3:5-8

TRUSTING GOD EVERYDAY

Honor the Lord with your possessions, and with the first-fruits of all your increase; so your barns will be filled with plenty, and your vats will over flow with new wine.   Proverbs 3:9-10

And your ears shall hear a word behind you, saying, this is the way, walk in it, when you turn to the right hand, and when you turn to the left.   Isaiah 30:21

For this reason I bow my knees to the Father of our Lord Jesus Christ, from whom the whole family in heaven and earth is named, that he would grant you, according to the riches of his glory, to be strengthened with might through his Spirit in the inner man, that Christ may dwell in your hearts through faith; that you being rooted and grounded in love, may be able to comprehend with all the saints what is the width and length and depth and height- and to know the love of Christ which passes knowledge; that you may be filled with all the fullness of God.   Ephesians 3:14-19

Now to him who is able to do exceedingly abundantly above all that we ask or think, according to the power that works in us, to him be glory in the church by Christ Jesus to all generations, forever and ever. Amen. Ephesians 3:20-21

Whosoever therefore shall confess me before men, him will I confess also before my Father which is in heaven. Matthew 10:32

And this is the record that God hath given to us eternal life, and this life is in his Son. He that hath the Son hath life; and he that hath not the Son of God hath not life. These things have I written unto you that believe on the name of the Son of God; that you may know that you have eternal life, and that you may believe on the name of the Son of God. 1 John 5:11-13

At that time Jesus answered and said, "I thank You, Father, Lord of heaven and earth, that you have hidden these things from the wise and prudent and have revealed them to babes. Even so, Father, for so it seemed good in your sight. All things have been delivered to me by My Father, and no one knows the Son except the Father, nor does anyone know the Father except the Son, and the one to whom the Son wills to reveal Him. Come to me, all you who labor and are heavy laden, and I will give you rest. Take my yoke upon you and learn from me, for I am gentle and lowly in heart, and you will find rest for your souls; for my yoke is easy and my burden is light. Matthew 11:25-30

God is spirit, and those who worship Him must worship in spirit and truth. John 4:24

Come now, and let us reason together, says the Lord; though your sins be as scarlet, they shall be as white as snow; though they be red like crimson, they shall be as wool. Isaiah 1:18

But God commends his love toward us, in that, while we were yet sinners, Christ died for us.
Romans 5:8

The Lord is near unto them that are of a broken heart; and saves such as be of a contrite spirit.
Psalm 34:18

And he (Jesus) must needs go through Samaria.
John 4:4

A woman of Samaria came to draw water; Jesus said unto her, "Give me to drink."   John 4:7

Therefore the Samaritan woman said to Him, "How is it that you, being a Jew, ask me for a drink since I am a Samaritan woman?" (For Jews have no dealings with Samaritans.)   John 4:9

The Samaritan woman's encounter
with God transformed her life.
She found God, the Living Water.
She found forgiveness, acceptance,
purpose, and her life was forever changed.

The Lord bless you and keep you; The Lord make his face shine upon you, and be gracious to you; The Lord lift up his countenance upon you, and give you peace.   Numbers 6: 24-26

Then said Jesus unto his disciples, if any one will come after me, let him deny himself, and take up his cross, and follow me.   Matthew 16:24

Are not five sparrows sold for two copper coins? And not one of them is forgotten before God. But the very hairs of your head are all numbered. Do not fear therefore; you are of more value than many sparrows.   Luke 12:6-7

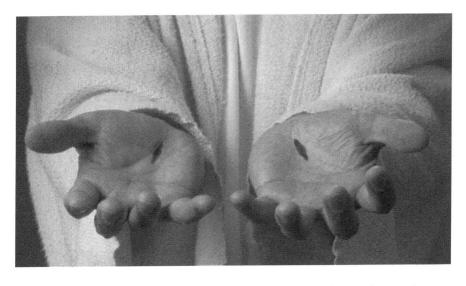

Can a woman forget her nursing child, and not have compassion on the son of her womb? Surely they may forget, yet I will not forget you. **See, I have inscribed you on the palms of my hands;** your walls are continually before me.   Isaiah 49:15-16

Therefore we do not lose heart. Even though our outward man is perishing, yet the inward man is being renewed day by day.   2 Corinthians 4:16

I, even I, am He who comforts you. Who are you that you should be afraid of a man who will die, and of the son of a man who will be made like grass?
                                        Isaiah 51:12

Oh give thanks to the Lord, for he is good, for his steadfast love endures forever!   Psalm 107:1

I have heard your prayers; I have seen your tears.
                                        2 Kings 20:5

For I the Lord your God will hold your right hand, saying unto you, Fear not, I will help you.
                                        Isaiah 41:13

DON'T LOOK BACK!
KEEP LOOKING FORWARD

"And Jesus said unto him, No man having put his hand to the plow, and looking back, is fit for the kingdom of God.   Luke 9:62

The two angels arrived at Sodom in the evening, and Lot was sitting in the gateway of the city.
                                              Genesis 19:1

As soon as they had brought them out, one of them said, "Flee for your lives! *Don't look back*, and don't stop anywhere in the plain!   Flee to the mountains or you will be swept away."
                                              Genesis 19:17

But Lot's wife, behind him, looked back, and she became a pillar of salt.   Genesis 19:26

Not that I have already obtained this or am already perfect, but I press on to make it my own, because Christ Jesus has made me his own. Brothers, I do not consider that I have made it my own. But one thing I do: forgetting what lies behind and straining forward to what lies ahead, I press on toward the goal for the prize of the upward call of God in Christ Jesus. Philippians 3:12-14

For I know the plans I have for you, declares the Lord, plans to prosper you and not to harm you, plans to give you a hope and a future.

Jeremiah 29:11

Remember not the former things, nor consider the things of old. Behold, I am doing a new thing; now it springs forth, do you not perceive it? I will make a way in the wilderness and rivers in the desert.

Isaiah 43:18-19

Remember Lot's wife. Whosoever shall seek to save his live shall lose it; and whosoever shall lose his life shall preserve it. Luke 17:32-33

"Therefore if any man be in Christ, he is a new creature: old things are passed away; behold, all things are become new." 2 Corinthians 5:17

Wherefore seeing we also are compassed about with so great a cloud of witnesses, let us lay aside every weight, and the sin which doth so easily beset us, and let us run with patience the race that is set before us.   Hebrews 12:1

Know you not that they which run in a race run all, but one receives the prize? So run, that you may obtain.   1 Corinthians 9:24

Let no man despise thy youth; but be thou an example of the believers, in word, in conversation, in charity, in spirit, in faith, in purity.
                    1Timothy 4:12

I sat watching as the old man slowly made his way toward me. I wondered who could he be, wondering have we met before; do I know him? As he got closer, I could see the brokenness, the emptiness in his face and eyes.

"Have you got one more, just one more?" He asked?

Tears filled my eyes, my heart ached for him, and I felt as empty as the trunk of my old vehicle where I kept devotionals and bibles. No sir I replied, I just gave the last one away, but I'll go get you one. I'll be right back. I went to get more bibles.

JESUS BEING BAPTIZED BY JOHN

OUTWARD EVIDENCE OF INWARD
CHANGE AFTER BEING BORN AGAIN

WATER BAPTISM

It came to pass in those days that Jesus came from Nazareth of Galilee, and was baptized by John in the Jordan.   Mark 1:9

Then Jesus came from Galilee to Jordan to be baptized by John, but John tried to deter him, saying, "I need to be baptized by you, and do you come to me?" Jesus replied, "Let it be so now; it is proper for us to do this to fulfill all righteousness," Then John consented. As soon as Jesus was baptized, he went up out of the water. At that moment heaven was opened, and he saw the Spirit of God descending like a dove and alighting on him. And a voice from heaven said, "This is my Son, whom I love; with him I am well pleased."
                                    Matthew 3:13-17

JESUS BAPTIZES BELIEVERS

RECEIVE THE

BAPTISM OF THE HOLY SPIRIT

BAPTISM OF THE HOLY SPIRIT

If ye love me, keep my commandments. And I will pray the Father, and he shall give you another Comforter, that he may abide with you forever; Even the Spirit of truth; whom the world cannot receive, because it seeth him not, neither knoweth him: but ye know him; for he dwelleth with you, and shall be in you. I will not leave you comfortless: I will come to you.   John 14:15-18

And it shall come to pass afterward, that I will pour out my spirit upon all flesh; and your sons and your daughters shall prophesy, your old men shall dream dreams, your young men shall see visions and also upon the servants and upon the handmaids in those days will I pour out my spirit.   Joel 2:28-29

And when the day of Pentecost was fully come, they were all with one accord in one place. And suddenly there came a sound from heaven as of a rushing mighty wind, and it filled all the house where they were sitting. And there appeared unto them cloven tongues like as of fire, and it sat upon each of them. And they were all filled with the Holy Ghost, and began to speak with other tongues, as the Spirit gave them utterance.   Acts 2:1-4

And did all drink the same spiritual drink: for they drank of that spiritual Rock that followed them: and that Rock was Christ.   1 Corinthians 10:4

For by one Spirit are we all baptized into one body, whether we be Jews or Gentiles, whether we be bond or free; and have been all made to drink into one Spirit.   1 Corinthians 12:13

In whom ye also trusted, after that ye heard the word of truth, the gospel of your salvation: in whom also after that ye believed, ye were sealed with that Holy Spirit of promise, which is the earnest of our inheritance until the redemption of the purchased possession, unto the praise of his glory.

Ephesians 1:13-14

PRAYER TO RECEIVE THE BAPTISM

Dear Heavenly Father,

I have asked You into my heart. I am Born Again. I want to be Baptized, Filled by Your Holy Spirit. I give myself wholly to you, Lord Jesus, and ask that you use me through the gifts of Your Holy Spirit to reach a world hurting, confused, lost, and in need of You. I love you Lord. Forgive me of my sins. I ask that You Baptize me in the Holy Spirit, in Jesus name I pray. Amen

Matthew 28:18-20

"Jesus came and spoke to them saying,
"All power is given unto me in Heaven and in earth.
Go ye therefore, and teach all nations, baptizing
them in the name of the
Father, and of the Son, and of the Holy Ghost:
Teaching them to observe all things whatsoever
I have commanded you:
and, lo, I am with you always, even
to the end of the world."
Amen."

THANKSGIVING

Give thanks in all circumstances; for this is the will of God in Christ Jesus for you. 1 Thessalonians 5:18

And whatever you do, in word or deed, do everything in the name of the Lord Jesus, giving thanks to God the Father through him.
Colossians 3:17

Do not be anxious about anything, but in everything by prayer and supplication with thanksgiving let your requests be made known to God.
Philippians 4:6

I will praise the name of God with a song; I will magnify him with thanksgiving.   Psalm 69:30

Let us come into his presence with thanksgiving; let us make a joyful noise to him with songs of praise!
Psalm 95:2

To you, O God of my father, I give thanks and praise, for you have given me wisdom and might, and have now made known to me what we asked of you, for you have made known to us the king's matter.   Daniel 2:23

When Daniel knew that the document had been signed, he went to his house where he had windows in his upper chamber open toward Jerusalem. He got down on his knees three times a day and prayed and gave thanks before his God, as he had previously.   Daniel 6:10

Therefore, as you received Christ Jesus the Lord, so walk in him, rooted and built up in him and established in the faith, just as you were taught, abounding in thanksgiving.   Colossians 2:6-7

For everything created by God is good, and nothing is to be rejected if it is received with thanksgiving, for it is made holy by the word of God and prayer.   1 Timothy 4:4-5

Therefore be imitators of God as dear children. And walk in love, as Christ also has loved us and given himself for us, an offering and a sacrifice to God for a sweet-smelling aroma. But fornication and all uncleanness or covetousness, let it not even be named among you, as is fitting for saints; neither filthiness, nor foolish talking, nor coarse jesting, which are not fitting, but rather giving of thanks.

Ephesians 5:1-4

For this you know, that no fornicator, unclean person, nor covetous man, who is an idolater, has any inheritance in the kingdom of Christ and God. Let no one deceive you with empty words for because of these things the wrath of God comes upon the sons of disobedience. Therefore, do not be partakers with them. Ephesians 5:5-7

For you were once darkness, but now you are light in the Lord, walk as children of light (for the fruit of the Spirit is in all goodness, righteousness, and truth), finding out what is acceptable to the Lord. And have no fellowship with the unfruitful works of darkness, but rather reprove them. For it is shameful even to speak of those things which are done by them in secret, but all things that are reproved are made manifest by the light, for whatever makes manifest is light. Ephesians 5:8-13

Therefore He says: "Awake, you who sleep, arise from the dead, and Christ will give you light." See then that you walk circumspectly, not as fools but as wise, redeeming the time, because the days are evil. Therefore do not be unwise, but understand what the will of the Lord is, and do not be drunk with wine, wherein is excess; but be filled with the Spirit, speaking to yourselves in psalms and hymns and spiritual songs, singing and making melody in your heart to the Lord, giving thanks always for all things to God the Father in the name of our Lord Jesus Christ, submitting to one another in the fear of God.   Ephesians 5:14-21

As the Father hath loved me, so have I loved you, continue in my love. If you keep my commandments, you shall abide in my love; even as I have kept my Father's commandments, and abide in his love.   John 15:9-10

Let not your heart be troubled: you believe in God, believe also in me. In my Father's house are many mansions; if it were not so, I would have told you. I go to prepare a place for you. And if I go and prepare a place for you, I will come again, and receive you unto myself; that where I am, there you may be also. And whither I go you know, and the way you know.   John 14:1-4

We ought always to give thanks to God for you brethren, as is right, because your faith is growing abundantly, and the love of every one of you for one another is increasing.   2 Thessalonians 1:3

I appeal to you therefore brethren by the mercies of God, to present your bodies as a living sacrifice, holy and acceptable to God, which is your spiritual worship.   Romans 12:1

The Lord repay you for what you have done, and a full reward be given you by the Lord, the God of Israel, under whose wings you have come to take refuge.   Ruth 2:12

There is therefore now no condemnation to those who are in Christ Jesus, who do not walk according to the flesh, but according to the Spirit. For the law of the Spirit of life in Christ Jesus has made me free from   the   law   of   sin   and   death.
                              Romans 8:1-2

For I am persuaded that neither death nor life, nor angels, nor principalities, nor powers, nor things present, nor things to come, nor height, nor depth, nor any other created thing, shall be able to separate us from the love of God which is in Christ Jesus our Lord.   Romans 8:38-39

"In a moment, in the twinkling of an eye, at the last trump: for the trumpet shall sound, and the dead shall be raised incorruptible, and we shall be changed."
1 Corinthians 15:52

SOON RETURNING KING

The Lord Himself will descend from heaven with a shout, with the voice of the archangel, and with the trump of God: and the dead in Christ shall rise first.
1 Thessalonians 4:16-17

You are worthy, O Lord, to receive glory, honor and power; for you have created all things, and for your pleasure they are and were created. Revelation 4:11

Worthy is the Lamb that was slain to receive power, and riches and wisdom and strength and honor and glory and blessing. Revelation 5:12

And every creature which is in heaven, and on the earth, and under the earth, and such as are in the sea, and all that are in them, heard I saying, Blessing and honor and glory and power be unto Him that sits upon the throne and unto the Lamb forever and ever. Revelation 5:13

Saying, Amen, Blessing, and glory and wisdom and thanksgiving and honor and power and might be unto our God for ever and ever. Amen.

Revelation 7:12

"Behold, I stand at the door, and knock: if any man hear my voice, and open the door, I will come in to him, and will eat with him, and he with me."

Revelation 3:20

For the Lamb who is in the midst of the throne shall feed them and lead them to living fountains of waters. And God shall wipe away all tears from their eyes.   Revelation 7:17

PRAYER

Dear God,

I have failed many times. You are a holy God. I am a sinner. I know I cannot come to Heaven as a sinner. I know I need a savior. I believe Your son, Jesus, was born to die for me. He died on the cross, giving His innocent blood as a ransom for my eternal soul. By accepting Jesus as my Savior, His blood washes away all of my sin.

Jesus, I ask you to forgive me of my sins, and come into my heart. Cleanse me and make me new.

Holy Spirit, fill my heart with the awareness of God's unconditional love, and give me power to be a witness.

I am now a Born Again Christian. Thank You God, for writing my name in The Lamb's Book of Life.

Amen

"Kingdom fingerprints should be left everywhere
we go and on everything we touch. How can I leave
a kingdom fingerprint on someone today?"
Rev. Chuck Sprouse

Kingdom Fingerprints

Kingdom Fingerprints is a non-profit organization dedicated to making the Word of God available to all. Every person we give a Bible is at a point of crisis. We share the Good News of Hope.

Touching Hearts – Changing Lives... Shares the love of Jesus Christ to elementary school children through Bible outreach ministry-making disciples. We share the message of God's love through Bible outreach, providing life-changing hope to those often neglected by others. We give out Bibles to the homeless, those suffering with addictions, mental health issues, debt, depression, loneliness, unemployment, abuse, and we pray with them to meet their needs. We have a responsibility to extend the hand of grace and mercy to the need on our own doorsteps.

To Order More Books:

BJStewart51@Gmail.com

To Make Donations and Contact:

Kingdom Fingerprints

P. O. Box 85

Ninety Six, S.C. 29666

Made in the USA
Columbia, SC
22 December 2022